BARRY ST. CLAIR

SPENDING TIME
ALONE WITH GOD

Chariot Books is an imprint of ChariotVictor Publishing,
a division of Cook Communications, Colorado Springs, Colorado 80918
Cook Communications, Paris, Ontario
Kingsway Communications, Eastbourne, England

Moving Toward Maturity Series

Following Jesus (Book 1)
Spending Time Alone with God (Book 2)
Making Jesus Lord (Book 3)
Giving Away Your Faith (Book 4)
Influencing Your World (Book 5)

Produced in cooperation with   REACH OUT MINISTRIES
                               3961 Holcomb Bridge Road
                               Suite 201
                               Norcross, GA 30092

All Bible quotations, unless otherwise indicated, are from the *Holy Bible, New International Version,* © 1973, 1978, 1984, International Bible Society. Used by permission of Zondervan Bible Publishers. Other quotations are from the *New American Standard Bible* (NASB), © the Lockman Foundation 1960, 1962, 1963, 1968, 1971, 1972, 1973, 1975, 1977; and from the *King James Version* (KJV).

Chapter opening and "Making It Personal" illustrations by Joe Van Severen.

Library of Congress Catalog Card Number: 83-61512
ISBN: 0-89693-292-3

                    9   10   Printing/Year   00   99   98   97

CONTENTS

SPECIAL THANKS

To Rod Minor, Debbie Hayes, the Reach Out Ministries office staff for working on this project with me.

To Randy Drake and Rob Lassiter for their creative artwork and design.

To Jane Vogel and the Victor Books team for their unceasing participation and unending patience.

To the youth ministers from across the country who have tested this material and given valuable suggestions.

To my wife Carol and my children Scott, Katie, Jonathan, and Ginny, who have loved me and encouraged me in my ministry.

To the Lord Jesus Christ for teaching me the things in this book.

A WORD FROM THE AUTHOR

Jesus Christ has made positive changes in my life. He can change your life too. And He can use you to change others!

Just make yourself AVAILABLE, and Jesus can:

 Help you know Him better.
Work in your life to make you a more mature Christian.
Motivate you to share Christ with others.
Use you to help other Christians grow toward maturity.
Make you a spiritual leader.

My goal for you is: "Just as you received Christ Jesus as Lord, continue to live in Him, rooted and built up in Him, strengthened in the faith as you were taught, and overflowing with thankfulness" (Colossians 2:6-7).

When that is happening in your life, then just as $2 \times 2 = 4$, and $4 \times 4 = 16$, and on to infinity, so Jesus can use you to multiply His life in others to make an impact on the world. How? One Christian (like you) leads another person to Christ and helps him grow to the point of maturity. Then the new Christian can lead another person to Christ and help him grow to maturity. And so the process continues. God gives you the tremendous privilege of knowing Him and making Him known to others. That is what your life and the Moving Toward Maturity series are all about.

The Moving Toward Maturity series includes five discipleship study books designed to help you grow in Christ and become a significant part of the multiplication process. *Spending Time Alone with God* is the second book in the series. The other books are:

Following Jesus (Book 1)
Making Jesus Lord (Book 3)
Giving Away Your Faith (Book 4)
Influencing Your World (Book 5)

God's desire and my prayer for you is that the things you discover on the following pages will become not just a part of your notes, but a part of your life. May all that's accomplished in your life be to His honor and glory.

Barry

PURPOSE

This book will help you develop a consistent, daily time alone with God. Learning to have fellowship with God through prayer and Bible study is basic for a disciple of Jesus Christ.

A disciple is a learner and a follower. As you learn to spend time alone with God, you will learn about Jesus Christ and how to follow Him. When you are learning about and following Jesus, you can agree with the Apostle Paul when he said:

> "[I am] confident of this, that He who began a good work in you will carry it on to completion [maturity] until the day of Christ Jesus" (Philippians 1:6).

Before you begin doing the Bible studies in this book, make the commitment to let Jesus Christ bring to completion all He wants to do in your life. Remember: God cares more about what is being developed in your life than about what you write in this book.

A helpful resource to assist you in spending time with God each day is the *The Time Alone with God Notebook*. Look for it at your local Christian bookstore, or write to Reach Out Ministries (address in the front of this book) for more information.

USES FOR
THIS BOOK

1. **GROUP STUDY** You can use this book as a member of an organized study group (Discipleship Family) led by an adult leader.* Each member of this group signs the commitment sheet on page 11, and agrees to use the book week by week for personal study and growth.

2. **INDIVIDUAL STUDY** You can go through this book on your own, doing one lesson each week for your own personal growth.

3. **BUDDY STUDY** You can ask a friend who also wants to grow to join you in a weekly time of studying, sharing, and growing together.

4. **ONE-ON-ONE DISCIPLESHIP** After you have mastered and applied each Bible study in this book to your own life, you can help another person work through his own copy of the book.

---

*The Leader's Guide for the *Moving Toward Maturity* series can be purchased at your local Christian bookstore or from the publisher.

PRACTICAL HINTS

(How to get the most out of this book)

If you want to grow as a Christian, you must get specific with God and apply the Bible to your life. Sometimes that's hard, but this book can help you if you will:

1. **Begin each Bible study with prayer**
   Ask God to speak to you.

2. **Use a study Bible**
   Try the *New International Version* or the *New American Standard Bible*.

3. **Work through the Bible study**
    Look up the Bible verses.
   Think through the answers.
   Write the answers.
   Jot down any questions you have.
   Memorize the assigned verse(s).
   (Use the Bible memory cards in the back of the book. Groups should select a single translation to memorize, in order to recite the verse[s] together.)

4. **Apply each Bible study to your life**
    Ask God to show you how to act on what you're learning from His Word.
   Obey Him in your relationships, attitudes, and actions.
   Talk over the results with other Christians who can encourage and advise you.

IF YOU'RE IN A DISCIPLESHIP FAMILY

➤ *Before* each group meeting, set aside two separate times each week to work on the assigned Bible study. If possible, complete the whole Bible study during the first time. Then during the second time (the day of or the day before your next group meeting), review what you've studied. This time should not be part of your time alone with God each morning. Do not use your time alone with God to work on your lesson.

➤ *After* you have discussed each Bible study with your Discipleship Family, complete the *Assignment* section of the study during the following week.

➤ Take your Bible, this book, and a pen or pencil to every group meeting.

PERSONAL COMMITMENT

I, _____ , hereby dedicate myself to the following commitments:

1. To submit myself daily to God and to all that He wants to teach me about growing as a Christian.

2. To attend all weekly group meetings, unless a serious illness or circumstance makes it impossible. If I miss more than one meeting, I will withdraw willingly from the group if it is determined necessary after meeting with the group leader.

3. To complete the assignments without fail as they are due each week.

4. To be involved in my local church.

I understand that these commitments are not only to the Lord but to the group and to myself as well. I will do my very best, with God's help, to completely fulfill each one.

Signed _____

1

GET TO KNOW HIM

Discovering time alone with God

Let's say you are in a dating relationship. How does it get to be a *relationship*? First you meet that special someone and are attracted to him (or her). Then because of the attraction, you want to get to know the other person better. So you begin to spend time with the other person, and the more time you spend together the better you get to know each other. Eventually the two of you develop a loving *relationship,* and as your love grows stronger, the time you spend together grows more special.

The same is true of your relationship with Jesus Christ. Once you have been introduced to Him, you begin the process of building a relationship with Him.

Just to see where you are right now in your relationship with Him, check the appropriate boxes below:

Yes No
☑ ☐ I have been introduced to Jesus Christ.
☑ ☐ I have accepted Him as my personal Savior.
☑ ☐ I am getting to know Him better.
☑ ☐ I am growing to love Him.
☐ ☑ I spend time with Him every day.
☑ ☐ I would like to know how to spend time alone with Him.
☑ ☐ I would like to improve the time I spend with Him.

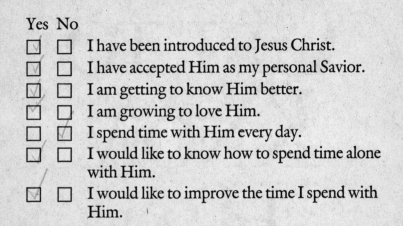

One of the secrets of all growing, dynamic Christians is that they consistently spend time alone with God.

If you could talk to Abraham, Moses, David, Paul, Martin Luther, John Wesley, Billy Graham, or any number of the great people of faith, they would all say that time alone with God was one of the strongest influences in their spiritual development. God wants you to be able to say the same thing.

But I go to church. What's so important about spending time alone with God? you may be thinking. That's like saying, "I see my boyfriend (or girlfriend) every day at school. Why do I need to date and be alone with him (or her)?" By spending time alone with Jesus Christ you can get to know Him on a much more personal, intimate level.

WHAT IS TIME ALONE WITH GOD?

1 Time Alone with God Is a Time of Personal Fellowship with the Lord
Getting to know Jesus Christ better and better should be a top priority for every Christian. When we spend time alone with Him, we get to know Him in a personal, intimate way.

How important was knowing Jesus Christ to the Apostle Paul? (Philippians 3:8)

He considered all things rubbish
and gave them up for the
sake of knowing and gaining
christ.

2 Time Alone with God Is When God Can Speak to You about Your Own Life
If you are like most young people, you're on the run all day long—class to class, friend to friend, appointment to appointment—and in between you have band or ball practice, chores at home, an occasional date, a part-time job, and plenty of homework. By the time you wade through your schedule, you hit the sack exhausted. But how often do you sit down just to take an honest look at your life? Do you take time to

evaluate where you are going and who you really are? A time alone with God helps you see yourself as He sees you.

During time with Him, God also shows you how to be more like Jesus. He does this in two ways:

(1) He lets you know *who you are not* as a Christian. He points out sins in your life, helps you admit them, and gives you the power to overcome them;

(2) God shows you *who you are*. He helps you discover the gifts He has given you and offers personal guidance so you can become the best person you can possibly be.

Write out the words of Psalm 139:23-24, and let them become a daily prayer from you to God.

search me, O God and know my heart;
test me and know my anxious thoughts
see if there is any offensive way in me,
and lead me in the way everlasting

 **3** **Time Alone with God Is a Time to Commit Your Day to the Lord**
Do you ever worry about tests, dates, family relationships, or your busy schedule? A time alone with God provides the opportunity to give all your worries to Him and trust Him to take care of you. You aren't big enough to handle every problem. God is!

How often should you commit your life, with all its worries and problems, to the Lord? (Luke 9:23)

Daily (take up the cross)
his

 **According to Proverbs 3:5-6:**

➡ What is one thing you shouldn't do?

lean on your own understanding

➡ What are two things you should do?

Trust the Lord with all your heart
in all your ways acknowledge him

➡ What will God do if you meet these conditions?

He will make your paths
straight

WHY HAVE A TIME ALONE WITH GOD?

1 **God Desires Your Fellowship**
You may not think you are important, but the God who made the oceans, mountains, stars, galaxies, and universe thinks you are somebody special. He receives pleasure from being with you!

Maybe you feel that reading the Bible and praying are things you _have_ to do — the duties of a "good Christian." No way! Prayer and Bible study are the communication channels between you and God. By using them to tune in to God, you can become His friend and have fellowship with Him.

We read in the Old Testament that "the eyes of the Lord move to and fro throughout the earth that He may strongly support those whose heart is completely His" (2 Chronicles 16:9, NASB).

What kind of people did Jesus say God is seeking? (John 4:23)

true worshippers who worship
the Father in spirit and in
truth

The exciting truth is that God *wants* to have fellowship with you. A close growing relationship with Jesus Christ brings joy to you and to Him.

2 Jesus Deserves Your Attention

As you fellowship with Jesus Christ, you soon realize that He had to pay an awesome price to make your relationship with God possible. Jesus was nailed to a splintered Roman cross. He shed His blood. He sacrificed His life. Why? Because there was no other way to bring you and God together, and Jesus loved you enough to pay that price.

Jesus deserves your attention. He is more than worthy of your praise, your love, your adoration, and your life. Spending time alone with God allows you to take your eyes off of yourself, and focus them on Jesus.

What should you do in response to Christ's sacrifice for you? (1 Corinthians 6:20)

Honor God with my body

3 The Holy Spirit Keeps Your Relationship with Jesus Growing

Sam was a regular kind of guy who was invited to a Christian youth conference. When he saw the crowd singing, praying, and sharing the excitement of being Christians, he committed his life to Christ right then and there. He was as high as a kite for the next couple of months, living in the warm glow of the decision he had made.

But then his girlfriend dumped him and *bam!* instant confusion. He no longer felt the love and peace of his previous commitment. All he could think was, *This Jesus Christ business just doesn't work like everybody says it does.*

Sam's reaction is common among Christians. Many people begin their Christian lives on cloud nine, only to hit the ground with a *thud* the first time something goes wrong. One main reason for their fall is the failure to develop a *daily* relationship with Jesus Christ.

Read Mark 1:35. Even Jesus, during His time on earth, actively sought fellowship with His Father.

When did Jesus seek fellowship with God?

early in the morning

Where did He go?

to a solitary place.

What did He do?

prayed

Because Jesus met alone with God regularly, He had the strength to do His Father's will even when He didn't feel like it physically or emotionally. (See Luke 4:1, 14.) If time alone with God was so desperately needed by Jesus, it should also be essential to you.

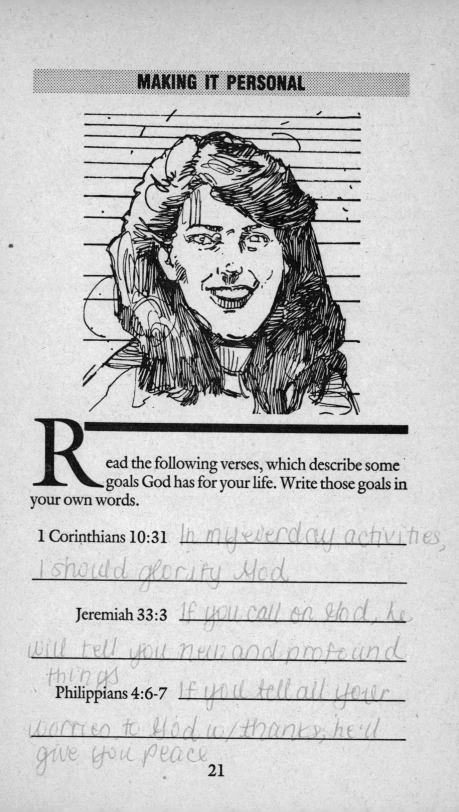

R ead the following verses, which describe some goals God has for your life. Write those goals in your own words.

1 Corinthians 10:31 _In my everday activities, I should glorify God_

Jeremiah 33:3 _If you call on God, he will tell you new and profound things_

Philippians 4:6-7 _If you tell all your worries to God w/thanks, he'll give you peace_

21

How can spending time alone with God *in Bible study* help you fulfill His goals for your life? (See Hebrews 4:12.)

It judges the thoughts + attitudes of my heart

How can spending time alone with God *in prayer* help you fulfill His goals for your life? (See Hebrews 4:16.)

find mercy + grace in my time of need

Review what you have learned in this Bible study, then answer these questions:

Why do I need personal fellowship with God?

To know his will, gain peace, He deserves it, develop a close relationship

Why do I need God to speak to me about my life?

I can't depend on what I think — only God can make my paths straight.

Why do I need a special time to commit every day to the Lord?

To remain strong even when adversity strikes.

Right now, choose a time to be alone with God for 15 minutes every day. During that time, read the assigned Scripture for the day (see *Assignment*), and talk with God in prayer. Be open to hearing what He wants to say to you. You may feel a little awkward at first, but soon this will become a special time for you.

Commit yourself to meeting alone with God every day at the time you have chosen. Then fill out the following commitment sheet.

Because I desire to glorify Christ in my life,

I, _____Diane Yeng_____
(name)

agree to have a daily time alone with God at

_____
(place)

and at _____
(time)

for the next 10 weeks.

Signature _____

Date _____

Complete this Bible study by memorizing Mark 1:35.

ASSIGNMENT
(NOTE: If you are a member of a Discipleship Family, do not complete this assignment until after your next meeting.)

1 Have a time alone with God for 15 minutes every day this week. Look up one of the following Bible passages each day. Spend about half of your 15 minutes thinking about what the verses mean, and how they apply to your life. Then spend the rest of your time talking to God in prayer.

Later sessions will give you more specific guidelines, but it's important for you to begin spending time with God now.

- ✔ Day 1: Philippians 3:8
- ✔ Day 2: Psalm 139:23-24
- ✔ Day 3: Proverbs 3:5-6
- ✔ Day 4: 2 Chronicles 16:9
- ✔ Day 5: John 4:23
- ✔ Day 6: Hebrews 4:12
- ✔ Day 7: Hebrews 4:16

2 Complete *Bible Study 2.*

BUILD THE RELATIONSHIP

Learning how to spend time alone with God

First date. The guy's sweaty palms finally get a firm hold on the telephone receiver. It only takes three wrong numbers before his nervous fingers dial the correct combination of digits. He has wanted to ask her out for weeks. On the other end the girl almost faints. She has wanted to go out with him for months. He has finally asked her, and she is trying not to show how excited she is.

Then come the details. Where will they go? What time? How will they get there? What are they going to talk about? All these questions are important, but number one on the list is: Are they going to like each other? *Everything else hinges on that basic relationship.*

How is your relationship with God? Is it growing, developing, bringing joy to you and to Him?

BUILDING BLOCKS

The whole concept of "building" something suggests work, and building a relationship is no exception. Look up the following verses and write the actions you need to take in order to build your relationship with God.

Matthew 6:33 _____

_____

Philippians 3:10 _____

_____

Matthew 22:36-38 _____

_____

After you build these three blocks in your relationship with God, other building blocks will naturally follow. For example, as you begin to love God, your love will be expressed in the following ways (be sure to look up each Bible reference and see how it relates to each area):

1 Prayer (Philippians 4:6-7)
As your love for God grows, you will want to let Him know. Prayer is your opportunity to talk to the Lord, tell Him what's on your mind, and listen for His answer.

2 Bible Study (John 14:23)
If you love God, you will want to know what He has to say to you. As you study the Bible, you will find practical advice from Him to you.

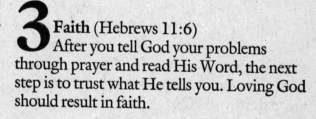

3 Faith (Hebrews 11:6)
After you tell God your problems through prayer and read His Word, the next step is to trust what He tells you. Loving God should result in faith.

4 Obedience (John 14:21)
You will want to obey what you know God is telling you. The Bible teaches that if you love God, you will keep His commandments.

Which of these four ways of expressing your love for God (prayer, Bible study, faith, obedience) do you need to develop most in your life? Why?

How can you start developing these areas today?

PLANNING A TIME ALONE WITH GOD

If you're planning to build a house, you need to gather wood, bricks, nails, and other specific materials. To build a relationship with God, a certain amount of preparation is also necessary.

1 **Choose a Time**
It is important to make a date with the Lord every day. Jesus often met with the Father in the morning (Mark 1:35), and His is a good example to follow. Have you ever seen a football team warm up *after* a game? Or a band warm up *after* a concert? Not a chance. In the same way, God wants you to warm up with Him *before* the action of your day begins. Why don't you try getting up early to spend time with Him?

Faithfully meet with God every day at the time that you choose. You may know what it feels like to be stood up on a date or to plan to meet someone and have him not show up. God understands and forgives your weaknesses, but He still wants you to make and keep your appointment with Him.

Remember, God desires fellowship with you.

Review the time you put on your "Time Alone with God Commitment" last week. Do you still feel that is the best time?

2 Choose a Place

It is usually much easier to communicate with God if you can be alone with Him in a place where you won't be distracted. Abraham talked to God in the desert, Moses on the mountaintop, and Daniel in the quiet of his room. Think of a good place for you to meet with the Lord, and write it here:

_____

3 Choose to Prepare

As you begin your time alone with God, your mental attitude is very important. Get up, shower, and get dressed. Don't set your alarm for 30 seconds before you are supposed to meet with the Lord, or you're likely to have a "time asleep with God." But you don't want to approach Him like a hummingbird in a hurricane either. Prepare your mind and come to God quietly and reverently.

What do the following verses have to say about your mental attitude?

Psalm 46:10 _____

_____

Isaiah 30:15 _____

_____

After you have prepared to meet with God, count on Him

to be there. He will provide some exciting surprises in your life when you meet with Him daily. Expect Him to respond as you reveal your thoughts to Him. God will meet you.

Special Hint: Set a goal for your time alone with God, a target that will keep you aimed in the right direction. Perhaps the best goal you could have would be to get to know Jesus Christ better. Think about Romans 8:29 and explain the phrase: "conformed to the likeness of His Son."

HOW TO GET STARTED
Here are some practical suggestions for starting a time alone with God. Use them to help you begin your daily devotional time.

Go to Bed on Time
You can't stay up late and then expect to wake up fresh the next morning. And you can't expect spiritual peace if you're a physical wreck.

Get Up in the Morning
Few young people are able to bounce out of bed with an enthusiastic, "Good morning, Lord!" Most of us would rather turn off our ringing alarm with a sledgehammer and go back to sleep. But with a little discipline and practice, you can become a cheerful early riser.

Keep a Journal
Record your thoughts, prayer requests, answers to prayer, and the things God shows you each day. You will soon

have an unbeatable source of inspiration as you look back and see the many things God has been doing in your life.

Look to Jesus

Don't start your day worrying about the bad things that might happen. Let your first conscious thoughts in the morning focus on Jesus Christ.

Don't Give Up

If you miss your time alone with God one morning, don't worry about it. You won't be a failure if you miss a day. He forgives you. Just try your best not to miss the next day.

Be Honest

If it feels like your time with God is empty and worthless, tell Him so. But don't quit. He would much rather have your honest complaints than your absence.

Be Consistent

Some of your times alone with God will be wonderful. Others will just be routine. But the way you *feel* is not always an accurate indicator of success. Every day that you spend time alone with the Lord will help you grow stronger, even if you don't sense the results right away.

 Read Jeremiah 29:13. The same promise that God made to Jeremiah years ago is still true for us today.

What will happen when you seek God?

_____

_____

How must you seek God?

_____

_____

It's time to get started! Don't worry if you don't yet know how to pray, what to pray for, or where to begin your Bible reading. This book is designed to walk you through these first steps in developing your daily time alone with God. The assignments for the next few weeks will start you on a regular plan of Bible study, and later you will focus on prayer.

Bible Study 3 will help you learn how to get the most from spending time in God's Word, but the following Bible Response Sheet will start you on the right track. (If you have completed *Following Jesus,* you will be familiar with this Bible study method.) The following sample is based on the first five verses of John 1.

BIBLE RESPONSE SHEET

DATE __5/10__

PASSAGE __John 1:1-5__

TITLE __Jesus brings light + life__

KEY VERSE __verse 4__

SUMMARY __the Word (Jesus)__
__(1) was in the beginning,__
__(2) was with God, (3) was__
__God, (4) made all things,__
__(5) was life, and (6) was__
__light__

PERSONAL APPLICATION __I need to let__
__Jesus be who He wants to be__
__to me. I can experience His__
__life + light by spending 15__
__minutes alone with Him every__
__morning for the rest of this__
__series of studies.__

Now try a Bible Response Sheet on your own, using John 1:6-8 as your reference passage. (You can make photocopies of the form on page 129 or copy the headings by hand in a notebook.) The *Application* is usually the hardest section, but it's also the most important. Notice that the one on page 35 was:

(1) *personal* — "To let Jesus be who He wants to be to me";

(2) *practical* — "I can experience His life and light";

(3) *measurable* — "By spending 15 minutes . . . every morning."

It may seem awkward to use the Bible Response Sheets at first, but it will become more natural with practice.

Complete this Bible study by memorizing 2 Timothy 3:16.

ASSIGNMENT

1 As you spend time alone with God every day this week, begin the habit of filling out a Bible Response Sheet for the Scripture you study. (This should take about 7 minutes.) Spend the rest of your 15 minutes in prayer.

- ✔ Day 1: John 1:9-14
- ✔ Day 2: John 1:15-18
- ✔ Day 3: John 1:19-28
- ✔ Day 4: John 1:29-34
- ✔ Day 5: John 1:35-42
- ✔ Day 6: John 1:43-51
- ✔ Day 7: John 2:1-11

2 Complete *Bible Study 3*.

LEARN THE WORD

Spending time in Bible study

E ating seems to be one of our nation's favorite pastimes. If you don't believe it, walk into the school cafeteria during lunch and watch the jocks compete in the Olympic food-stacking competition. First, they try to see who can pile the most food on a normal-size plate. Then, with their quivering conglomerations in hand, they do a balancing act back to their tables.

Because eating is such an obsession, dieting is also a popular pastime. Diets are supposed to be practical and good for you, but sometimes they get a little crazy. Most of them have catchy names, so you need to read the fine print. The

"Tropical Diet" might sound exotic, but after a week of only mangoes, kumquats, and kiwi fruit, your stomach feels like a monsoon. Another ever-popular diet is the "Seefood Diet"—you see food; you eat it.

But perhaps none of today's diets are as unusual as that of the Prophet Jeremiah, thousands of years ago. What did he enjoy feasting on? (Jeremiah 15:16)

_____

_____

Just as food gives strength to your physical body, the regular intake of God's Word keeps you spiritually strong. Without regular Bible "meats," you can't expect to be all God wants you to be. Before you read any farther, stop now and ask the Lord to give you the same desire for His word that Jeremiah had. It's a diet everyone should follow.

WHY SPEND TIME IN GOD'S WORD?

1 You Will Get to Know Yourself Better

Read Hebrews 4:12 and note the effect that the Bible can have on different areas of your life. How do you think God's Word affects:

➡ your "soul" (personality)?

_____

_____

➡ your "spirit" (that relates uniquely to God)?

_____

_____

➡️ your "thoughts" (mind)?

_____

_____

➡️ the "attitudes of the heart" (motivation)?

_____

_____

Think about one specific area of your life that the Word of
God needs to "penetrate." Describe it below.

_____

_____

Letting God's Word touch our lives is like having a skillful
surgeon use his scalpel to carefully remove any cancerous
growths that threaten our well being. God uses His Word
to remove the things in our lives that are keeping us from
being all He wants us to become.

2 You Will Get to Know Jesus Better
Who is the focus of God's letter, the
Bible? (John 5:39)

_____

_____

What is one thing about Jesus that you want the Bible to help you understand better?

_____

_____

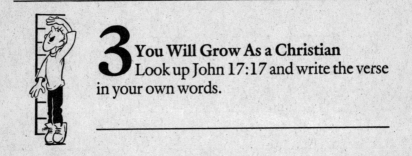

3 You Will Grow As a Christian
Look up John 17:17 and write the verse in your own words.

_____

_____

_____

Now think about the meaning of this verse, using the following definitions.

➤ Sanctify: to set apart for God's purposes
➤ Truth: the reality that underlies everything in life

When Christ prayed that you would be "sanctified by the truth," He was praying that you would become more like Him.

 God's Word (the Bible) is truth. Look up these passages and write down one or two key words from each passage to support the fact that the Bible is trustworthy.

Psalm 119:160 _____

_____

Luke 1:1-4 _____

_____

2 Timothy 3:16 _____

_____

2 Peter 1:16 _____

_____

1 John 1:1-3 _____

_____

But just knowing that God's Word is the truth won't automatically make you grow as a Christian. What else do you need to do? (1 Peter 2:2)

_____

_____

Just as babies need milk to help them grow into healthy adults, Christians need God's Word to help them mature into men and women of God.

 **4 You Will Have a Successful Life** Read Psalm 1:1-3. What makes a person ultimately successful or "blessed"?

_____

_____

> "blessed" means "happy"
> "counsel" is "advice"

What are your different sources of "counsel"? List them below, and note whether or not each source provides you with good advice.

_____

_____

_____

_____

_____

What is the Bible called in verse 2?

_____

Use a dictionary to record the definition of "meditate."

_____

_____

_____

_____

When a person meditates on God's Word daily, he will be like a "tree firmly planted" (NASB). List three results of being firmly planted (v. 3).

_____

_____

_____

_____

5 You Will Be Able to Handle Temptation

If you are like most people, you face strong temptations. God's Word can prepare you to face them. As you spend time in Bible reading, God will direct you to helpful verses, such as 1 Corinthians 10:13:

"No temptation has seized you except what is common to man. And God is faithful; He will not let you be tempted beyond what you can bear. But when you are tempted, He will also provide a way out so that you can stand up under it."

Bible study gives you the ammunition to handle any situation the way Jesus would handle it. (See Matthew 4:1-11.)

**God wants you to know
His Word because:
You will get to know yourself better.
You will get to know Jesus better.
You will grow as a Christian.
You will have a successful life.
You will learn to handle temptation.**

45

PREPARING TO STUDY GOD'S WORD

Sometimes studying the Bible is like trying to eat lobster with only your fingers. You know there's plenty of delicious, mouthwatering meat just waiting to be devoured, but you can't quite break the shell that surrounds it. So, as you begin to put some serious time into Bible study, try to collect some tools that can help you "get to the meat" of it:

 Bible. It's important to have a Bible that you can easily read and understand. You might want to use one of the more recent translations for this purpose.

Bible Dictionary. This is an alphabetical listing of biblical people, places, terms, and other background information you wouldn't learn from just reading the Bible itself.

English Dictionary. You'll probably run across some words that aren't familiar to you. Look them up as you go along.

Bible Atlas. This tool can help you with the geography of the Bible.

Commentaries. These are books that explain and interpret the Bible — verse by verse or section by section.

**Always keep in mind:
The Bible is not just literature
to be studied or facts
to be learned.
It is truth to be applied.**

Now just a few reminders to make your time alone with God more profitable for you:

As much as possible,

 Stick to the time you've chosen to meet with God.

 Study the Bible for *personal* meaning, not for how it applies to others.

 Be willing to let the Holy Spirit change you.

 Fill out a Bible Response Sheet *every day*. Keep the ones you have completed in a notebook, so you will have a record of your spiritual growth.

Read "How to Study a Passage of Scripture" on page 128. Then use Psalm 1 to practice the observation, interpretation, application, and memorization method of Bible study. List any new insights from this psalm that might be of help to you this week.

Complete this Bible study by memorizing Joshua 1:8.

ASSIGNMENT

1 Follow this Bible reading schedule during your daily 15-minute time alone with God. Fill out a Bible Response Sheet and spend time in prayer each day.

   ✔ Day 1: John 2:12-17
   ✔ Day 2: John 2:18-25

✔ Day 3: John 3:1-8
✔ Day 4: John 3:9-17
✔ Day 5: John 3:18-24
✔ Day 6: John 3:25-36
✔ Day 7: John 4:1-14

2 Complete *Bible Study 4*.

4

HIDE
THE
WORD

Spending time in Scripture memory

It's been a long day, but it's finally over and all of your favorite shows are on TV. After three hours of prime-time pleasure, you joyfully discover that the late-late show is one you've been wanting to see (so you do). You even stay up for the national anthem. But as you see the words "Test Pattern" on the screen, your groggy mind recalls the phrase "Test tomorrow." Then comes the shocking realization that you have a math test first thing in the morning.

You race to your room, fling open your book, and start learning the equations. You've been over the material in class, so you have some idea of what to do. But those formulas are all so much alike!

Three hours later, you can say the equations in your sleep (and you do). Naturally, you wake up late the next morning and get to school just before the bell rings. Your test is waiting for you on the desk. You read the first question and know exactly where the needed formula is in the book, *but you can't think of it.* You work the problems you can, and spend the rest of the time wondering how you will explain your low grade to your parents.

Sound familiar? All of us have faced similar situations when we weren't as well prepared as we should have been. We've studied, but we just can't remember what we've learned. The same thing often happens with the Bible.

It's good to read the Bible and even better to study it carefully. But if you stop there, you won't be any more ready for the emergencies of life than you were for the imaginary math test! You need to memorize God's Word.

During biblical times, Jewish men wore *phylacteries* during prayer. Phylacteries were small leather boxes that contained Scriptures written on slips of parchment.

One box was attached by straps to the left arm (to be near the heart), and another was placed right between the eyebrows. These men literally carried God's Word with them. (Some Jews still wear phylacteries during their prayer time.)

You don't have to wear little leather boxes, but you *can* carry God's Word with you all the time.

 Read Proverbs 6:20-23. How can you take God's teachings with you?

_____

_____

What will be the results when you do?

_____

_____

BENEFITS OF SCRIPTURE MEMORY

1 **The Bible Will Come Alive for You**
Scripture memory brings new life into your Bible study. Read Psalm 19:7-14.
According to verses 7-9, God's Word:
➤ Revives your soul (v. 7).
➤ Is a source of truth and wisdom (v. 7).
➤ Is a source of joy and enlightenment (v. 8).
➤ Endures forever (v. 9).
➤ Is always sure and righteous (v. 9).

What are some other advantages of Scripture memory, based on verses 10-14?

_____   _____

_____   _____

_____   _____

2 **You Will Gain Strength to Face Everyday Situations**
Obviously, you can't study the Bible all day long. But when

you carry its teachings in your mind and heart, you can recall those truths when you need them. How is God's Word described in Ephesians 6:17?

_____

_____

Scripture memory allows you to carry your "weapon" with you all the time.

3 You Will Prosper Spiritually
Last week, you examined a passage that compares a person who meditates on God's Word daily with a tree firmly planted (Psalm 1:1-3, NASB). Try to recall from memory the three results of being "firmly planted." Then look back at *Bible Study 3* if you need help.

_____

_____

_____

4 You Will Have Strength to Overcome Temptation
We have already seen that *studying* the Bible can help you handle temptation. But how can *memorizing* Scripture help you even more?

_____

_____

Look at Psalm 119:9-11. What did David say about memorizing Scripture?

_____

_____

5 You Will Become a More Effective Witness for Jesus Christ

Knowing God's Word will give you confidence to witness. According to Psalm 119:12-13, what will you do when you know God's Word?

_____

_____

6 You Will Begin to See Things from God's Perspective

When you "hide God's Word in your heart," you begin to think the way God wants you to. How does this change in thinking take place? (Romans 12:2)

_____

_____

YOU CAN MEMORIZE SCRIPTURE

In spite of the many benefits that Scripture memory offers, you might be thinking, *It's no use. It sounds good, but I have a lousy memory.* Before you give up, try this simple experiment:

What's your name? Address? Phone number? Where do you go to school? What classes are you taking? What are your teachers' names?

Your Memory Is Good!

You learn dates for history class. You remember how to get to your friends' houses. And if that "special" person lets you know that he/she has a birthday coming up, you're sure to remember the date. Anything is easy to remember if you're interested in it and use it enough.

Your Attitude Makes a Difference

Memorizing is a developed skill that can be improved. Adopting an attitude of *confidence* and *desire* will help you learn. Read Psalm 119:127-131. What words in this passage show you that David had a desire to know God's Word?

_____

_____

_____

What are some of the reasons that you desire to know God's Word?

_____

_____

_____

You Have What You Need

You have "everything [you] need for life and godliness" (2 Peter 1:3). That includes the ability to remember what God wants you to remember. What has Jesus promised you? (John 14:26)

_____

_____

_____

Fill in the following blanks and make these a faith statement to God:

✔ I can memorize Scripture because _____

_____

_____

✔ I can memorize Scripture because _____

_____

_____

✔ I can memorize Scripture because _____

_____

_____

STEPS TO SCRIPTURE MEMORY

1 **Pray**
Every time you begin to memorize Scripture, remember to pray in "3-D." Ask God to help you:

➤ *Decide* to memorize.
➤ *Desire* to do it.
➤ *Delight* in doing it.

2 Plan

If memorizing Scripture doesn't come naturally to you, the plan on page 130 can make memorization easier. Turn there now before going further in this Bible study. Read each step carefully, and make sure you understand it before continuing.

**Remember:
Scripture memory takes
discipline.**

3 Practice

Now that you have a plan, put it into practice. Continue to memorize the verse(s) you are assigned each week. *Don't try to do too many at first.* Remember to review each verse every day for at least 30 days.

Find a friend to memorize Scripture with, and practice your verses on each other every week. Hold each other accountable for learning new verses and reviewing the ones you've already memorized.

4 Persist

Work on your verses every day. Don't give up. Review! Review! Review! That's the only way to remember the verses.

**Inch by inch, it's a cinch.
Yard by yard, it's hard.**

Beware of certain traps that might get you off the track in your Scripture memory. Watch out for:

➡ Spiritual pride—don't let it get you when you've learned a few verses.
➡ Overload—don't take on too much at one time.
➡ Procrastination—don't put it off.
➡ Burnout—don't quit.

S pend some time right now going through the steps you have just learned, and memorize Psalm 119:9-11. When you finish, review all the verses you have memorized so far. Continue to do this *every* day. Make sure you know each verse word perfect.

ASSIGNMENT

1️⃣ Continue your daily time alone with God. Fill out a Bible Response Sheet for each day:

- ✔ Day 1: John 4:15-26
- ✔ Day 2: John 4:27-38
- ✔ Day 3: John 4:39-54
- ✔ Day 4: John 5:1-16
- ✔ Day 5: John 5:17-24

✔ Day 6: John 5:25-35
✔ Day 7: John 5:36-47

2 Review all the verses you have memorized so far.

3 Be sure to spend time in prayer every day this week, because prayer is the topic of the next session.

4 Complete *Bible Study 5*.

TALK WITH GOD

Spending time in prayer

It's 6 A.M. Your alarm rings, and your first impulse is to catch another hour's sleep before school. But you've promised God that today you will start getting up earlier in order to spend some time with Him. It would be a lot easier to spend time with God at the Church of the Inner Spring (mattress, that is) under the warm protection of Reverend Sheets. But you figure your snoring isn't what the psalmist meant by "make a joyful noise." So how do you convince yourself to get up and keep your commitment to the Lord?

The first step is to have a proper understanding of prayer.

Some people act like prayer is a chore, much like taking out the garbage. It's something they don't really enjoy doing, but they do it anyway to keep the air clear. (They figure God will be satisfied if they go through an occasional prayer ritual.)

But prayer *should* be the combination that unlocks the door to all the riches of the kingdom of God. Failure to pray is the barrier which keeps that door shut. On the other hand, the consistent practice of prayer will open wide the door of God's work in your life.

THE PURPOSE OF PRAYER

As you pray, you discover: (1) who God is, (2) what God wants you to do, and (3) how He wants you to do it. Through prayer you learn to converse with God. As you talk with Him, you get to know Him on a personal level. And soon you will discover that you have the power you need to do whatever God asks you to do.

Read John 14:12-14. What kind of power results from prayer?

_____

_____

What does Jesus promise to give you when you pray?

_____

According to John 16:24, what is a major reason for not receiving answers to prayer?

_____

Sometimes we don't even bother to ask God for the things we want, and then we complain when we don't get them. In an average week, about how much time do you spend in *personal* prayer?

_____

Do you feel like you're spending enough time in prayer, or would you like to spend more?

MOTIVATION FOR PRAYER

Douglas Thornton was a student who saw the positive effect that time alone with God was having on some of his classmates. Thornton had a lot of trouble getting up every morning, but he was determined to begin each day by spending time with God.

His strong motivation wouldn't let him give up. He finally built a device from a fishing pole, four hooks, and an alarm clock. When his alarm clock rang in the morning, the pole would be released to pull on the four hooks, which were attached to the four corners of his sheets. Once the covers were pulled off the bed, it wasn't so hard for him to get up. Sounds pretty ridiculous, doesn't it? That is, until you ask the question: "How much did Douglas Thornton want to know God?" He wanted to know God enough to do anything—even to look a little ridiculous.

Why should you pray? What should you ask for? Are there conditions you must meet in order to obtain an answer? What are the results of prayer? Until you know, you may not have a strong motivation to pray.

 What encouragements to pray can you discover in the following passages?

John 15:7-11 _____

_____

James 5:13-16 _____

_____

2 Chronicles 7:14 _____

_____

Matthew 6:5-13 _____

_____

Matthew 26:41 _____

_____

Maybe you've made past commitments to pray more often, only to forget or taper off again. That may be because you don't have a real desire to pray. Your commitment should be a *result* of your motivation (desire) to meet with God. If you have no inner desire to meet with Him, you're much less likely to honor your commitment to Him. But if you really want to know God better, you'll find a way to spend time alone with Him in prayer every day.

GOD'S ANSWERS TO PRAYER

God wants to give us the things we need as we pray for them. But prayer is not like a quarter spent in a vending machine to automatically get what we want. God wants us to have what will be best for us. Prayer involves:

(1) putting ourselves in the position to know God;
(2) receiving what God has to give us; and
(3) doing what He wants us to do.

God never lets your prayers go unanswered. When you ask God for something, He will respond to your request in one of three ways:

1 He Might Say YES
When you pray for something according to God's will, He promises an affirmative answer. He loves you and wants to answer yes to your prayer requests.

What confidence can you have when you ask God for something? What is the condition to His saying yes to your request? (1 John 5:14-15)

_____

_____

2 He Might Say WAIT
Sometimes He has a good reason for not giving you what you ask for right away. You may not always understand why He chooses to let you wait, but you can be sure that He is doing what is best for you.

What is one reason God might have you wait for an answer to prayer? (James 1:2-4)

_____

_____

What attitude should you have if God tells you to wait?
(Psalm 27:13-14)

_____

_____

 **3** **He might say NO**
Just as good parents must sometimes
say no to their children's requests, God must
also refuse our prayer requests from time to
time.

What did David want to do, and why did God
say no? (1 Chronicles 22:7-10)

_____

_____

What request did Paul make that God refused? (2 Corinthians 12:7-10)

_____

_____

What is another reason the Lord might refuse to answer a
prayer? (James 1:6-8)

_____

_____

_____

Think of one prayer in your past when God said yes, one

when He said wait, and one when He said no. Be specific.
Looking back, can you see why He answered those prayers
in the ways He did?

_____

_____

_____

THE PROMISES OF PRAYER

God's Word provides hundreds of promises
pertaining to prayer. Look up the following
passages to discover how they apply to you
personally. Then begin to claim them in your
time alone with God.

The Promise	What It Means to Me
Matthew 7:7-8	_____
	_____
James 1:5	_____
	_____
Philippians 4:19	_____
	_____
Philippians 4:6-7	_____
	_____

DIFFERENT ASPECTS OF PRAYER

So far, this Bible study has been about prayer in general. But there are different aspects of prayer. What you have learned so far in this study applies to all of them, but each aspect of prayer has a slightly different purpose.

The Scriptures that follow should give you some indication of the different kinds of prayer. Look up the passages and then try to describe the purpose of each element of prayer in your own words.

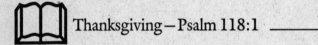 Praise—Hebrews 13:15 _____

_____

_____

_____

_____

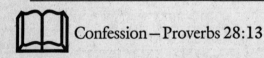 Thanksgiving—Psalm 118:1 _____

_____

_____

_____

_____

Confession—Proverbs 28:13 _____

_____

_____

_____

_____

📖 Petition—John 16:23-24 _____

_____

_____

_____

📖 Intercession—1 Timothy 2:1-2 _____

_____

_____

_____

_____

Spend a few minutes now evaluating your prayer time with God. In what ways does your prayer life need development?

_____

_____

What can you do to improve it?

_____

_____

_____

Now spend some time in prayer. Tell the Lord about your desire or lack of desire to pray and ask Him to empower and motivate you toward a consistent prayer life.

Complete this Bible study by memorizing John 15:7.

ASSIGNMENT

1 Continue your daily Bible reading. Fill out a Bible Response Sheet for each day.
- ✔ Day 1: John 6:1-14
- ✔ Day 2: John 6:15-21
- ✔ Day 3: John 6:22-31
- ✔ Day 4: John 6:32-43
- ✔ Day 5: John 6:44-52
- ✔ Day 6: John 6:53-63
- ✔ Day 7: John 6:64-71

2 Complete *Bible Study 6*.

3 Begin to familiarize yourself with the Prayer Action Sheet (on page 131). You will soon be learning how to use this sheet to get more from your prayer time.

REMINDER: You should be spending 15 minutes alone with God each day. Spend the first 7 minutes doing your Bible reading and Bible Response Sheet, and use the rest of the time to talk to God in prayer.

PRAISE THE LORD!

Spending time in praise

How do you feel when the coach says the top 20 people will make the basketball team, and you're number 21?

Or when everybody but you gets a date to homecoming?

Or when your dad gets a new job, and you have to move away from all your friends?

Everyone faces problems and disappointments from time to time, but people react differently to difficult circumstances. List your three biggest problems below, and briefly explain how you are handling each one. (What emotions do you feel? What actions are you taking?)

Problem   How I Am
                                 Responding

_____   _____

_____   _____

_____   _____

Now read 2 Samuel 21:15-22, and look at the problems that David had to face. His problems were giants (literally)! Once, in the thick of battle, David became weak and exhausted. He looked up and saw a giant bearing down on him with a new sword and an eight-pound spear. But David's men rescued him and killed the giant.

Later in the war, David's men killed three more giants. One, who was thought to be the brother of Goliath, carried a spear as big as a 4' x 6' board. Another giant had six fingers on each hand and six toes on each foot. Talk about huge, ugly problems!

How did David handle *his* "giants"? Check it out in 2 Samuel 22:1-7. How did David feel during his struggles? (vv. 5-6)

_____

_____

How did he overcome his negative feelings? (vv. 4, 7)

_____

What did David do after his battle? (v. 1)

David's initial response was to ask God's help and then to *praise* Him. Praise may be the single most important ingredient in prayer. It is an open response of your love for God — expressing back to Him the qualities that are true of Him, and adoring Him for who He is. Praise was a natural response for David — even during times of trouble.

RESPONDING WITH PRAISE

This diagram portrays a common response to problems.

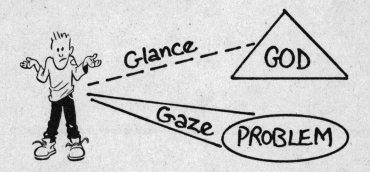

When a problem arises, you think, *God, why did You do this to me?* You begin to concentrate your thoughts, energy, and feelings on the problem. Then anxiety and fear begin to plague you.

When Peter was walking on the water to meet Jesus, why did he begin to sink? (Matthew 14:30)

There is a better way to deal with problems. The following diagram is based on Philippians 4:6-7: "Do not be anxious about anything, but in everything, by prayer and petition, with thanksgiving, present your requests to God. And the peace of God, which transcends all understanding, will guard your hearts and your minds in Christ Jesus."

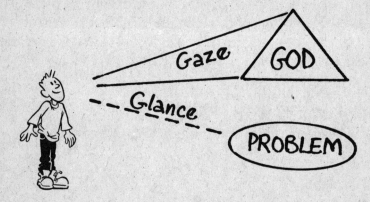

GAZE: to stare at continuously
GLANCE: to take a quick look

So when a problem comes up, you can say, "God, You are sufficient to take care of this situation. I trust You. I praise You." When you respond with praise, you can experience the peace of God.

PRAISE: HOW TO DO IT

One of the greatest meals ever invented is the "potluck" supper. Every family prepares a dish to bring to put with all the other families' dishes. If no one prepares ahead of time, the supper might consist of 10 bags of Doritos. But when everyone prepares and brings something different, it's the best meal in town.

Praise works in much the same way. For it to be the most meaningful, you need to prepare several different "dishes" ahead of time.

Read Psalm 105:1-5. This passage suggests several things you should bring with you as you prepare to praise the Lord. See how many you can discover without looking ahead. Then compare your findings with the following list.

_____

_____

_____

_____

Bring Thanksgiving
"Give thanks to the Lord" (Psalm 105:1). Come before God with an attitude of thanks. Without an "attitude of gratitude," it's hard to praise the Lord. Thank God for one thing He has given you, and write it here.

_____

_____

Bring Your Voice
"Call on His name" (Psalm 105:1). To *call* is to speak to God aloud. Practice this part of your praise right now by

saying, "I praise You, Lord." Say it aloud as you write it below.

_____

_____

Bring Your Testimonies

"Make known among the nations what He has done" (Psalm 105:1). Think back to some of the wonderful things God has done for you. Tell Him how you have seen Him work in your life in the past, and list examples below. Praise Him for each of those times He has been there when you needed Him.

_____

_____

_____

_____

Bring Your Songs

"Sing to Him" (Psalm 105:2). Sing a song out loud to God, even if you only sing it in the shower. Think of a song to start practicing on, and write the title below.

_____

Bring Adoration

"Glory in His holy name" (Psalm 105:3). Read Isaiah 9:6. Meditate on the names for God that are listed there, and praise Him for one that is especially meaningful to you. In the space below, write the name and the reason you chose it.

_____

_____

Bring a Seeking Attitude

"Let the hearts of those who seek the Lord rejoice. Look to the Lord and His strength; seek His face always" (Psalm 105:3-4).

 Seek Him rejoicing.
Seek His strength.
Seek His presence.

If you continually seek God, you will be able to praise Him even when you face difficult situations. Read James 1:2-4. Then think of a problem you are currently struggling with. In the space below, praise God that He is using that problem to make you spiritually strong.

_____

_____

Bring Your Bible

"Remember the wonders He has done" (Psalm 105:5). Look in God's Word and then praise Him for His mighty acts. Psalms 145–150 are excellent examples of praise. Read Psalm 147 and write out your praise to God as you go along.

_____

_____

_____

_____

_____

_____

MAKE IT MEANINGFUL

Follow these suggestions to praise the Lord in the most meaningful way.

1 **Express Your Praise Aloud to God**
If other people are around, find a place where you can be alone, or just whisper.

2 **Learn to Praise Spontaneously**
At first, you might only echo passages from the Bible that offer praise to God. But soon you should feel praise arising from your own heart.

3 **Continue to Praise the Lord Even If You Feel Awkward at First**
As you get used to praising Him, praise will become an enjoyable part of your time alone with God.

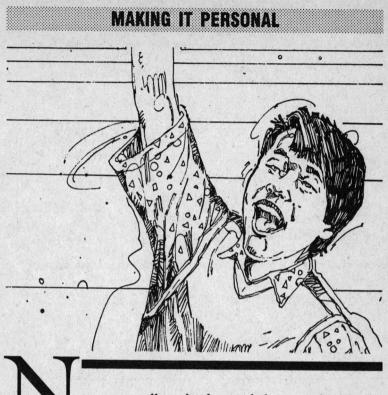

N ow to put all you've learned about praise into practice, let's "walk through" a sample passage. Then you can do one on your own.

Scripture passage: "The Lord is my strength and my song; He has become my salvation. He is my God, and I will praise Him, my father's God, and I will exalt Him" (Exodus 15:2).

My response: "Lord, I praise You that You are my strength and my song. Because of that, I know I can face today with joy and confidence in You. Thank You, Father, that Jesus has become my salvation. His death on the cross made possible my relationship with You. I praise You in Jesus' name."

Prayer Action Sheet (*Praise* section only): See page 131.

PRAYER ACTION SHEET

Date _10/15_____

PRAISE:
Write down one reason to praise the Lord today.

Lord, I praise You that You are the one who gives me strength.

Now go through the same process with 2 Samuel 22:2-4.

My Response: _____

_____

_____

PRAYER ACTION SHEET

Date _____

PRAISE:
Write down one reason to praise the Lord today.

_____

_____

Complete this Bible study by memorizing Psalm 146:1-2.

ASSIGNMENT

1️⃣ Continue daily Bible reading during your time alone with God. Fill out a Bible Response Sheet each day.

- Day 1: John 7:1-9
- Day 2: John 7:10-20
- Day 3: John 7:21-31
- Day 4: John 7:32-39
- Day 5: John 7:40-53
- Day 6: John 8:1-11
- Day 7: John 8:12-24

2️⃣ Make praise a part of your daily prayer life. To get started, begin with these verses. Complete the *Praise* section of the Prayer Action Sheet after each reading.

- Day 1: Psalm 8
- Day 2: Psalm 23
- Day 3: Psalm 34:1-3; 50:1-6
- Day 4: Psalm 63:1-4; 66:1-7
- Day 5: Psalm 67
- Day 6: Psalm 84
- Day 7: Psalm 86

Additional verses to help you praise God in the future times alone with Him are listed on page 132.

3️⃣ Complete *Bible Study 7.*

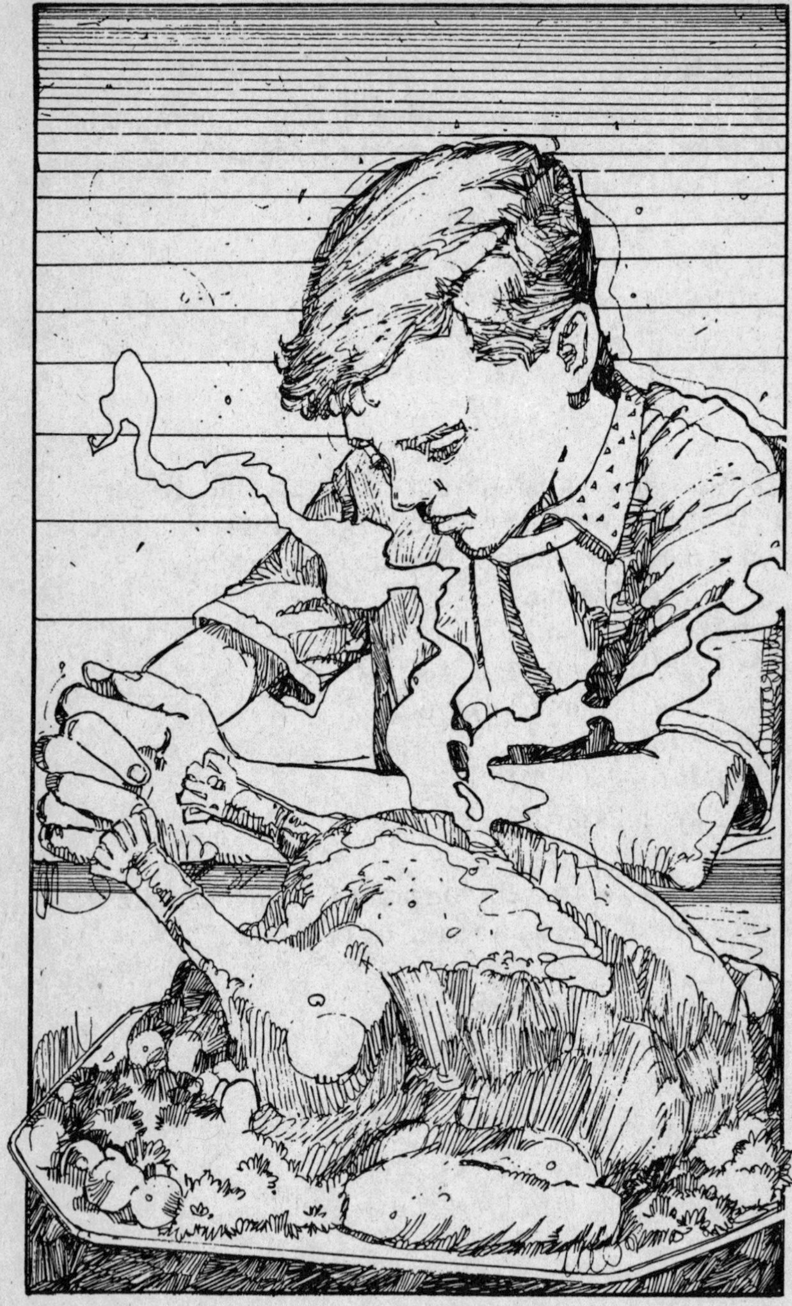

GIVE THANKS

Spending time in thanksgiving

It's finally Christmas morning. You've been on a continual shopping spree since the Labor Day sales, looking for just the right gift for each member of your family. The big moment comes; the wrapping paper flies; and you wait to hear all the glowing comments of gratitude.

"Oh. A chartreuse sweater. I guess they were out of navy."

"I already have an electric shoestring-lacer."

"This *Ant Farming through the Ages* book looks . . . nice. I'll put it on the shelf and read it later."

"I think this Mold-O-Matic penicillin-maker will work better in the attic."

Four months of hard work and not one "thank you"! It's a lousy feeling to go out of your way to do something special for someone and then see that they don't appreciate it.

God's gifts to us are "good and perfect" (James 1:17). Think how He must feel when we don't bother to say thanks for what He has given us.

KEYS TO GIVING THANKS

Giving Thanks: an Attitude
Our lack of thankfulness can be downright embarrassing. Consider the example recorded in Luke 17:11-19. Jesus came near the 10 men who had leprosy, a disease that eats the skin. Lepers were outcasts during Bible times, because the disease was so contagious. But Jesus had compassion on these men. He healed them and instructed them to go to the priests and be declared clean again. Only one of the men took the time to tell Jesus "thank You."

What attitude did this man have that Jesus noticed?

_____

_____

Why do you think the other nine didn't say thanks?

_____

_____

Jesus wanted the lepers to realize that *the giver is more important than the gift*. But only 1 out of 10 got the message.

If you had been one of those lepers, would you have been the one who said thanks or one of the other nine? Why?

_____

_____

Giving Thanks: Entering In
In Psalm 100 we are told to "enter [God's] gates with thanksgiving" (v. 4). Read the psalm and write your reflection below.

_____

_____

Suppose the following people knocked on your door and wanted to come in. Would you let them?

YES	NO	
☐	☐	A thief
☐	☐	An encyclopedia salesman
☐	☐	A member of a strange cult
☐	☐	A friend
☐	☐	Your dad

Your willingness to let them into your home probably depends on what kind of relationship you have with each of them. The better you know the person the more likely you are to let him enter.

How can you enter God's gates? Isaiah 22:22 refers to "the key to the house of David." But who holds the key to the house? (Revelation 3:7-8)

You can "enter His gates" if you know and walk with Jesus Christ. As you enter His gates, you should enter with thanksgiving (Psalm 100:4). Over and over again, the Bible teaches us to give thanks.

 Look up each of these verses and summarize them: Psalm 7:17; 92:1; 107:1; 118:1, 29.

_____

_____

Psalm 100 also instructs us to praise God. Both praise and thanksgiving bring pleasure to God, are essential to prayer, and are natural responses to knowing God. They are very similar, so take a closer look to see how they are different.

Praise:

- Adores God for who He is.
- Worships His ways.
- Honors His character.

Thanksgiving:

- Appreciates what God has done.
- Expresses gratitude for His works.
- Honors His actions and gifts.

If you are a guy, your marriage vows will say, "I take thee to be my lawful wedded wife." You wouldn't say, "I take thee to be my lawful wedded cook," because "cook" only describes one thing your bride does. It isn't an accurate description of _who she is._ After you are married, you will _thank_ her for cooking good meals, and you will _praise_ her for being your wife.

The same distinction is true of your relationship with God. You _praise_ God for _who He is,_ and you _thank_ Him for _what He does._

Giving Thanks: Working It Out
List some of the good things that God has given you. Look around right where you are and write down the things that come to mind.

_____

_____

_____

_____

If you lost everything on the above list in the next 24 hours, could you still give thanks to God for your circumstances?

_____

If things are tough for you now, take heart. Job was a man who lost everything he had—his health, wealth, friends, and even his family. But God still wanted Job to give Him thanks because of who He is and what He had done.

Read Job 38:4-18. What was God trying to get Job to realize?

_____

_____

In the midst of all Job's problems, God wanted Job to express gratitude. What did Job finally discover about giving thanks? (Job 42:2)

_____

A New Testament version of what Job learned can be found in 1 Thessalonians 5:16-18. Read the passage and write down what the Apostle Paul had to say about thanksgiving.

_____

_____

What difficulties in your life make it hard for you to give thanks?

_____

_____

Right now, as a faith statement of thanks (like Job and Paul expressed) complete the following sentences:

I can give thanks for . . .

_____

_____

I can give thanks when . . .

_____

_____

If we know what God is really like, we can thank Him for every circumstance.

GOD IS ...

Reread Psalm 100. List any words that describe what God is like. Then compare your list with the one that follows.

_____

_____

_____

The Lord Is Our Creator

"It is He who made us" (Psalm 100:3). Check out Genesis 1:1, 27-28, and Psalm 139:13-16. What kind of Creator is God?

_____

_____

"The Lord Is Good" (Psalm 100:5)

What would you do if someone gave you a million dollars?

__ 1. Spit in his face.

__ 2. Yawn and say you could take it or leave it.

__ 3. Thank him and say, "What can I do for you?"

What good things do you miss out on when you seek God? (Psalm 34:8-10)

_____

How should you respond to God's goodness? (Psalm 34:1-3)

93

_____

_____

The Lord Is Loving

"His love endures forever" (Psalm 100:5). This idea, appearing 240 times in the Old Testament, is a major theme of the Bible. Because He loves you, God is personally committed to you, even when you fail to love Him.

How much is God's love worth? (Psalm 63:3)

_____

_____

The Lord Is Faithful

"His faithfulness continues through all generations" (Psalm 100:5). You can trust God because He is always reliable.

Read the following verses and then write your own definition of faithfulness:
Numbers 23:19, Lamentations 3:22-23, 2 Thessalonians 3:3, and 2 Timothy 2:13.

Faithfulness = _____

_____

Martin Reinhart was a German pastor who lived during the Thirty Years War. In 1636, he buried 5,000 people who had lived in his community (an average of almost 14 per day). In spite of the war, pestilence, and heartache, he wrote this table blessing for his children:

Now thank we all our God,
With heart and hands and voices,
Who wondrous things hath done,
In whom His world rejoices,
Who from our mothers' arms
Hath led us on our way
With countless gifts of love,
And still is ours today.

**Because God's character
is consistent, we will never
face a situation for which
we cannot thank Him.**

Think about *your* problems, disappointments, and heartaches. List them here, thanking God for each one.

_____

_____

_____

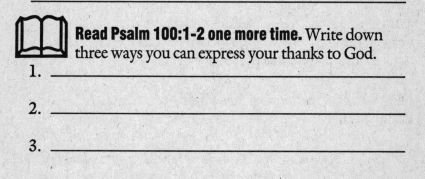 **Read Psalm 100:1-2 one more time.** Write down three ways you can express your thanks to God.

1. _____

2. _____

3. _____

Now let's walk through an example of how you can begin to give thanks during your time alone with God. Using Psalm 84:11 as a text, first *read through* the verse, and then *pray through* the verse to express your thanks to God in a personal way.

Here's an example of how you might "pray through" Psalm 84:11:

> *"Lord, I thank You that You are my shield. That means I can count on You to protect me as I try to patch up a relationship with a friend who is angry at me."*

Then, after praying through the verse, fill out the *Thanksgiving* section of the Prayer Action Sheet:

One reason I can thank God today:

> *Lord, I give you thanks that you will protect me as I face my angry friend.*

Now turn to the "Seven Days of Thanksgiving" on pages 132–134, and work through the first day's Scripture on your own.

To complete this Bible study, memorize 1 Thessalonians 5:18.

ASSIGNMENT

1 Continue daily Bible reading, using Bible Response Sheets.
- Day 1: John 8:25-36
- Day 2: John 8:37-46
- Day 3: John 8:47-59
- Day 4: John 9:1-7
- Day 5: John 9:8-25
- Day 6: John 9:26-41
- Day 7: John 10:1-6

2 Study one of the "Seven Days of Thanksgiving" each day this week, and begin to complete the *Thanksgiving* section on your daily Prayer Action Sheets. (To complete the *Praise* section, you will want to continue the "Thirty Days of Praise" on page 132.)

3 Complete *Bible Study 8*.

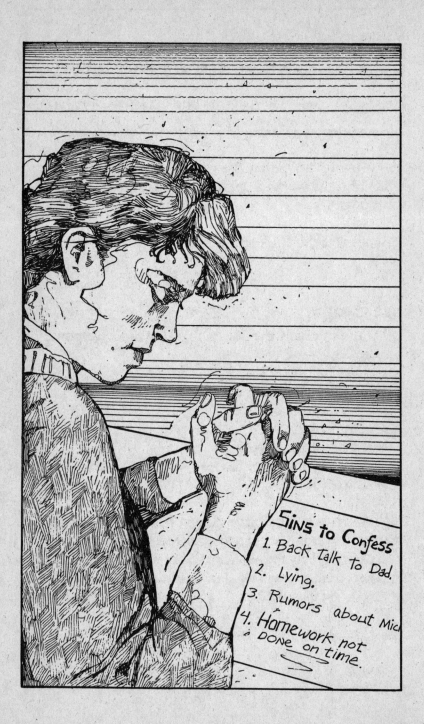

LIVE CLEAN

Spending time in confession

Can you remember doing something wrong as a little kid, and then trying to keep your parents from finding out? Maybe you broke your mother's vase and hid the pieces, hoping she wouldn't notice. But you felt like a criminal. And every time your parents walked past the bare spot where the vase used to be, your heart skipped a beat. You sensed that they sensed something was wrong, and you became uncomfortable around your own parents. Before long you began to wish they *would* find out.

When your folks finally discovered your cover-up, they either said, "Accidents happen. Don't you know we love you more than that old vase?" or they disciplined you and said, "That was an expensive antique. Next time be more careful." But either way, you were suddenly *free!* When you no longer had to live with guilt, you discovered a wonderful feeling of relief.

It would have been easier to have confessed in the first place. But children don't understand that confession leads to freedom. Unfortunately, neither do many adults.

How about you? When you sin against God, do you try to hide your sin? Or do you quickly confess?

Confessing sins is easier than trying to hide them!

WHAT DOES IT MEAN TO CONFESS YOUR SINS?

Everyone needs to know about confession. Why? Because God is a holy God who hates sin. While man is sinful, he cannot be in God's presence. The Bible says that "All have sinned and fall short of the glory of God" (Romans 3:23). The Bible also teaches that the result of sin is death—eternal separation from God. (See Romans 6:23.) So if everyone has sinned, and the result of sin is spiritual separation from God, it might seem that no one can have a right relationship with God.

But because of God's love for us, He provided a way to bring us back to Him. The sacrifice of His Son bridged the gap between man and God. Jesus' death on the cross made a right relationship possible. Write out the following verses in your own words.

1 Peter 3:18 _____

_____

_____

Ephesians 1:7 _____

_____

It is through confession that you claim God's forgiveness for sin. "If you confess with your mouth, 'Jesus is Lord,' and believe in your heart that God raised Him from the dead, you will be saved" (Romans 10:9).

But that fact of confession is only the beginning. Confession is still important after you have accepted Jesus Christ. You will continue to sin, and you will need to receive God's forgiveness for those sins. So after you become a Christian, confession means that you (1) *agree* with God when you do wrong, and (2) *accept* His forgiveness that has already been provided for you through Jesus' death.

HOW DO YOU CONFESS YOUR SINS?

 **Agree With God**
If you're like most people, our definition of *confess* is to tell or admit something to someone (like telling your parents you broke their vase). But in the Bible, the Greek word translated as *confess* means "to agree with" or "to acknowledge." So when you know that you are guilty, you reply, "You are right, Lord. I confess (agree)." Then you experience His forgiveness for your sin.

In order to confess your sin, you need to *see yourself from God's perspective.* That means you need to get rid of your *pride.*

101

Psalm 51 is an example of confession. David had committed adultery with Bathsheba and then arranged a battle strategy that would "accidentally" kill her husband. This psalm was written as he came to the Lord confessing his sins of adultery and murder—some pretty heavy charges.

What attitudes did David ask God to have toward him? (v. 1)

1. _____

2. _____

What did David ask God to do for him? (v. 2)

1. _____

2. _____

Against whom did David sin? (v. 4)

_____

How did David agree with God about his sin? (v. 4)

_____

The first step of confession is to agree with God that:

1. **What you did was wrong.**
2. **Jesus Christ already paid the price of your sin when He died on the cross.**
3. **You will turn away from your sins.**

Accept Forgiveness
When Christ died, He provided forgiveness for you. And when you confess any sins in your life, you can accept His forgiveness over and over again. That might not mean a lot to you until you realize the extent of God's forgiveness.

 According to Psalm 103:12, how far away from you does God remove your sin?

_____

_____

God forgives you for:
sins in the past.
sins in the present.
sins in the future.

 Read Isaiah 53:4-6. Now picture your sin as a huge rock on your shoulders, weighing you down. You would remove it if you could, but it is too heavy for you. Then imagine Christ lifting the rock and placing it on His own shoulders. Why is Jesus qualified to take away your sin and put it upon Himself?

_____

_____

 Read Psalm 51 again and list some of the positive results that you can experience from receiving God's forgiveness through confession.

103

verse 2 _____

verse 7 _____

verse 8 _____

verse 10 _____

verse 12 _____

verse 13 _____

verse 14 _____

verse 15 _____

Confession is the key that unlocks the door of God's forgiveness, taking away your sin and guilt.

The second part of confession is accepting God's forgiveness and its results.

HOW TO EXPERIENCE A CLEAN LIFE

God forgives your sin — no matter how bad it is. The wonderful thing about confession is that He also takes away the guilt along with the sin. You are free!

Check out God's promise to you in 1 John 1:9. Rewrite the verse in your own words as it relates to sins you have committed.

_____

Do you have sins that need to be confessed? Right now, confess them to the Lord and claim God's forgiveness for them. Be specific. Write your prayer here.

_____

_____

_____

Thank God for cleaning those sins out of your life. Then make confession a daily habit. You *can stay clean all of the time!*

1 **Prepare Your Heart**
Meditate on these verses from Psalm 139:23-24: "Search me, O God, and know my heart; test me and know my anxious thoughts. See if there is any offensive way in me, and lead me in the way everlasting."

2 **Search Your Heart**
You can do this by first reading God's Word, and then by asking yourself, "Does the Scripture point out a sin in my life?"

3 **Confess Your Sin**
Remember, to confess means simply "to agree with God." So agree with God in prayer, and then receive His forgiveness.

4 **Claim God's Promise**
Take what God says in His Word about you, and pray that it will become true in your life.

On pages 135–136 is a section titled "Thirty Days of Confession" which is divided into two parts: *Sins to Confess* and *Promises to Claim*. You'll be using this section during the next week, so let's "walk through" the first day's assignment.

Under *Sins to Confess* for Day 1 (page 135), you'll find the reference verse, 2 Timothy 2:22, and the question, "Do you have impure thoughts?" After reading the verse and considering the question, your prayer of confession might be something like this:

"Lord, I confess that I do have impure thoughts. Specifically, I sometimes have fantasies that are lustful and thoughts You would not be proud of."

Then turn to Day 1 of the *Promises to Claim* section (page 136), and read the verse(s) you find there. Here's how you might claim the promise from Philippians 4:8:

> *"Lord, I claim from Philippians 4:8 that I can think about You and praise You to get rid of my impure thoughts and fantasies."*

If your sin is against God, confess it to God and make things right with Him.

If your sin is against another person, confess it to God and make things right with the other person.

If your sin is against a group, confess it to God and make things right with the group.

Complete this Bible study by memorizing 1 John 1:9.

ASSIGNMENT

1 Fill out a Bible Response Sheet each day.
- ✔ Day 1: John 10:7-18
- ✔ Day 2: John 10:19-30
- ✔ Day 3: John 10:31-42
- ✔ Day 4: John 11:1-16
- ✔ Day 5: John 11:17-27
- ✔ Day 6: John 11:28-44
- ✔ Day 7: John 11:45-57

2 Study one of the "Thirty Days of Confession" (pages 135–136) during your time alone with God each day this week. Complete the *Confession* section of your daily Prayer Action Sheet. If you have time, continue to fill out the *Praise* and *Thanksgiving* sections.

3 Complete *Bible Study 9*.

"Personal Prayer Requests"
1. Help with Grades
2. Patience with Mom + Dad
3. Dating
4. Be more Like Jesus
Do my Chores
6. Take care of my room

PRAY FOR YOURSELF

Spending time in petition

Hey, Mom! I'm starving. Do you have a piece of bread I can munch on until breakfast is ready?"

"No, Dear, but here's a rock. It has nine essential minerals."

"Uh, I think I'll pass. How long till the eggs are ready?"

"We're not having eggs today. I've fixed you a nice plate of scorpions — good eating if you can catch them without get ting stung."

"I just remembered — I'm starting my diet today. I think I'll skip breakfast. By the way, did you pick up those new fish for my aquarium?"

"I started to, Dear, but the pet shop had the cutest assortment of baby rattlesnakes, so I got them instead. I put them in your room. I'm surprised you haven't found them by now."

This conversation sounds like it may have come from an old "Twilight Zone" script, but it is actually based on the words of Jesus Himself (Matthew 7:9-10; Luke 11:11-12). What was Jesus saying? Loving parents want to give their children what they ask for, so long as it is good for them. They don't substitute dangerous or harmful gifts for good ones.

Neither does God. He wants us to have the good things we ask for, so we should let Him know what we need. That process of asking for our needs is called *petition*.

The last three Bible studies were devoted to praise, thanksgiving, and confession — aspects of prayer that are centered around your response to God. Hopefully these three ingredients of prayer have helped you to know God better. Now you are ready to begin exploring how God responds to you. As you go to Him with your petitions, He supplies what you need. Jesus taught that asking for things in prayer is very important.

 Read Matthew 7:7-8. In this passage, what three commands does Jesus make? (v. 7)

_____

_____

_____

What three promises does He make? (v. 8)

_____

_____

_____

 **PETITION: ASKING**
Picture this: all God has to give is stored in a huge, inexhaustible tank. Imagine that He has a large channel flowing out of that tank into your life. At the end of the channel there is a valve that controls the flow of the channel. Petition is what turns that valve so that what God has can flow to you.

When we ask God to supply the things we need, there are certain attitudes and conditions He expects of us.

What specific guidelines for petition are given in the following Bible references?

Matthew 21:22 _____

_____

John 15:7 _____

_____

James 4:2-3 _____

_____

John 16:23-24 _____

What do you think it means to ask "in Jesus' name"?

_____

_____

Praying "in Jesus' name" simply means that you pray according to the character and purpose of Jesus. In other words, what He desires for you should be the same thing you desire to see Him do in your life.

PETITION: THE PROMISES

When God makes a promise, it can't be broken. The Bible is full of God's promises to His followers. Look up the following verses; briefly record the promises given there; and describe what each promise means to you personally.

John 14:12-14 _____

_____

_____

_____

Ephesians 3.20 _____

_____

_____

_____

Philippians 4:19 _____

_____

_____

_____

1 John 5:13-15 _____

_____

_____

_____

"Seven Days of Petition" (pages 136–137) includes more promises you can begin to claim as you pray this week. Study them; apply them to your life; and begin to explore the exciting dimension of prayer—*petition*.

PETITION: FINDING GOD'S ANSWERS

Did you ever have the type of math book that had all the answers in the back? If so, did you always wait until you had worked the problem to check on the answer? No way. First you'd sneak a peek at the right answer, then work on the problem until it came out right.

That's how you should pray. God's promises are like the answers in the back of the math book. He wants you to know them ahead of time. When a problem comes along, solving it is often just a matter of finding the right "answer" (promise).

When you know God's "answers," your praying takes on a

113

new dimension. *The Bible becomes your answer book!*

When you ask God for something:
➤ Believe that God will answer you.
➤ Be specific in what you ask.
➤ Claim God's promises.
➤ Ask in Jesus' name. (Pray that Christ will give you what He wants you to have.)
➤ Ask with proper (unselfish) motives.
➤ Write down your request.
➤ Listen and watch for the answer.

In the space below, make a list of the things you often worry about.

_____

_____

_____

According to Philippians 4:6-7, how should you handle those worries?

_____

_____

List the things you have asked God for recently.

_____

_____

If God gave you everything on your list, would you have a little or a lot? Why?

_____

Name one specific prayer request you have.

_____

_____

_____

Review the promises listed in this chapter, and study the ones in the "Seven Days of Petition" section (pages 136–137). Does one of the promises apply to your request? If so, write it below. If not, ask God to show you one that does apply.

_____

_____

To complete this Bible study, memorize Matthew 7:7-8.

ASSIGNMENT

1️⃣ Continue daily Bible reading. Fill out a Bible Response Sheet each day.
  ✔ Day 1: John 12:1-9
  ✔ Day 2: John 12:10-22

✔ Day 3: John 12:23-33
✔ Day 4: John 12.34-43
✔ Day 5: John 12:44-50
✔ Day 6: John 13:1-17
✔ Day 7: John 13:18-30

2   Study one passage each day from the "Seven Days of Petition" section (pages 136–137), and begin to complete the *Petition* section of your daily Prayer Action Sheets. If you have time, continue to fill out the *Praise, Thanksgiving,* and *Confession* sections.

Also begin a "Record of Petition" (see page 138 for a sample). Then you will be able to keep up with your requests and God's answers.

3   Complete *Bible Study 10.*

10

PRAY FOR OTHERS

Spending time in intercession

Let's say a friend of yours at school has a severe drug problem. He wants to overcome it, but he just can't seem to quit. He has tried counseling, special medication, and "cold turkey" withdrawal, but nothing has worked so far. Now he comes to you. What difference can you make in his situation?

Or perhaps another friend is not married, but pregnant. She just found out and doesn't know what to do. She is certain that when she tells her folks, they will throw her out of the house. The baby's father wants nothing to do with her. What can *you* do to help?

119

Maybe the problem is closer to home. What if your parents fight all the time and are thinking of divorce? What can *you* do to help keep them together?

At first glance, you might not think you could do anything in these situations. But you *can* call on God for help with your friends' or parents' problems. *He* is able to do something. The process of asking God's help on the behalf of someone else is called *intercession*.

Hopefully, you have begun to recognize the power of prayer during the past several weeks. As a result, your relationship with God should be stronger. Your *praise* and *thanksgiving* glorify and please God. *Confession* allows you to maintain a clean life. *Petition* lets you receive God's provision for your needs. But *intercession* reaches beyond your one-to-one relationship with God, and begins to include other people.

HOW INTERCESSION WORKS

As you pray for others, God releases His Holy Spirit into the world. The Holy Spirit can be anywhere instantly, and can penetrate even the toughest defense barriers. What are you able to do with the help of the Holy Spirit? (2 Corinthians 10:3-5)

_____

_____

So don't give up. If you've tried to reach out to others, only to have them build "walls" around themselves, try intercession. The Holy Spirit will eventually break down those walls and overcome the other person's stubborn resistance. Many times *your* intercessory prayer can be the first important step that releases God's Spirit into someone's life.

An example of intercessory prayer is found in Colossians 1:9-12.

Who wrote this passage, and to whom? (See Colossians 1:1-2.)

_____

How often did the author intercede for these people?

_____

What did he ask God to do for them?

_____

_____

_____

HOW TO INTERCEDE: SOME BASIC GUIDELINES

Pray with Confidence That God Will Answer
How can God's promise in 1 John 5:14-15 help you develop confidence?

_____

_____

Pray Persistently

Don't give up if you don't see immediate results. The person you are praying for will sometimes have strong defenses that prevent him from responding right away. It may take persistent prayer to wear down those "strongholds."

How did Samuel feel about persistent prayer? (1 Samuel 12:23)

_____

_____

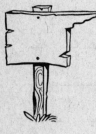

Pray in Agreement with Other People

Pray with friends or relatives who share your concern for the person you are praying for. When you read Matthew 18:18-20, what clues do you find about the value of praying in agreement with other people?

_____

_____

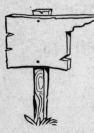

Pray with the Assurance That No Problem Is Too Big for God to Handle

Study Ephesians 3:20-21. What is God's promise about handling big problems through you?

_____

**Your prayers + God's power
= positive changes
in the lives of others**

STEPS TO EFFECTIVE INTERCESSORY PRAYER

In addition to the basic guidelines on intercession, here are some suggestions to get you started and help you follow through.

Be Specific

Ask the Lord to give you specific people and situations to pray for. Don't try to pray for everyone every day. But be sure to pray for those whom God brings to your mind. Read John 14:12-14. What does Jesus want to do through you?

What do the words *whatever* and *anything* say to you about being specific in your prayers?

Take Authority over Satan

The devil will interfere with intercessory prayer whenever he can. How can you avoid his destructive influence? (James 4:7)

Concerning Satan's power, what has God promised?
(1 John 4:4)

_____

_____

Expect Results
Don't be surprised to see God do great things. Read Acts
12:1-17. What did the church ask God to do?

_____

_____

How did God answer their prayers?

_____

_____

How did they respond to His answer?

_____

_____

How do you think this incident affected the people's ability
to trust God in the future?

_____

_____

O n page 139 is a form that will help you keep track of your prayers for others. Right now, take a few minutes to think about the people you need to pray for regularly (family members or close friends). Then fill out a form for each person you think of. (You can photocopy the one in this book or write your own.) Make a couple of extra pages to record the names of others you pray for less frequently.

Keep these sheets. Be sure to record God's answers to your prayers. Like the people in Acts who prayed for Peter, seeing God answer specific prayers will build your faith.

If you have trouble thinking of things to pray for someone else, the "Prayers You Can Pray for Others" sheet on page 140 will get you started.

Complete this Bible study by memorizing 2 Corinthians 10:4-5.

ASSIGNMENT

1️⃣ Begin the *Intercession* section on your Prayer Action Sheet and from now on complete the entire Prayer Action Sheet each day.

2️⃣ Continue your daily time alone with God, using the Bible reading and prayer guidelines you have learned in this book. Below is the breakdown for the rest of the Book of John.

John 13:31-38	John 16:23-28	John 19:23-30
John 14:1-7	John 16:29-33	John 19:31-37
John 14:8-14	John 17:1-8	John 19:38-42
John 14:15-21	John 17:9-19	John 20:1-10
John 14:22-31	John 17:20-26	John 20:11-18
John 15:1-8	John 18:1-14	John 20:19-23
John 15:9-16	John 18:15-27	John 20:24-31
John 15:17-21	John 18:28-40	John 21:1-14
John 15:22-27	John 19:1-12	John 21:15-19
John 16:1-11	John 19:13-22	John 21:20-25
John 16:12-22		

FOR FUTURE TIME ALONE WITH GOD

After you have completed this Bible study, continue to spend 15 minutes with God each day: 7 minutes in Bible study (using the verses above) and 8 minutes in prayer (using the ingredients of praise, thanksgiving, confession, petition, and intercession).

The next book in the Moving Toward Maturity series is titled *Making Jesus Lord*. It will take you further in the process of Christian discipleship.

By the time you finish this book, your daily time alone with God will include Bible study, praise, thanksgiving, confession, petition, and intercession. Here is a guideline that will allow you to include all aspects of Bible reading and prayer within a 15-minute period of time.

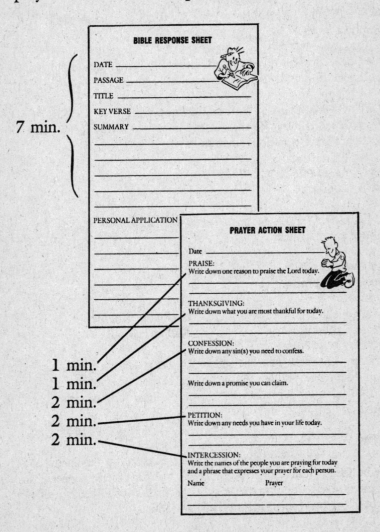

7 min.

BIBLE RESPONSE SHEET

DATE _____

PASSAGE _____

TITLE _____

KEY VERSE _____

SUMMARY _____

PERSONAL APPLICATION

1 min.
1 min.
2 min.
2 min.
2 min.

PRAYER ACTION SHEET

Date _____

PRAISE:
Write down one reason to praise the Lord today.

THANKSGIVING:
Write down what you are most thankful for today.

CONFESSION:
Write down any sin(s) you need to confess.

Write down a promise you can claim.

PETITION:
Write down any needs you have in your life today.

INTERCESSION:
Write the names of the people you are praying for today and a phrase that expresses your prayer for each person.

Name   Prayer

HOW TO STUDY A PASSAGE OF SCRIPTURE

OBSERVATION (Use with *Title* and *Key Verse* sections of your Bible Response Sheet.)

Pray first for the Holy Spirit's guidance, and then read the passage carefully. Read with an open mind, ready to receive and obey what God has to teach you.

INTERPRETATION (Use with the *Summary* section of your Bible Response Sheet.)

Step One — Read the verses preceding and following the passage in order to understand the proper setting and context.

Step Two — Ask yourself these questions about the passage: *Who? What? When? Where? Why?* and *How?* Write down your insights and any unanswered questions you may have.

Step Three — Look up unfamiliar terms in a standard dictionary or a Bible dictionary.

APPLICATION (Use with the *Personal Application* section of your Bible Response Sheet.)

Step One — Look for:
Promises to claim   *Commands* to obey
Attitudes to change   *Actions* to take
Challenges to accept   *Examples* to follow
Sins to confess   *Skills* to learn

Step Two — Describe how the passage applies to your life by asking yourself these questions: "How can I make this passage personal?" "How can I make it practical?" "How can I make it measurable?" Be specific.

MEMORIZATION
Find a verse or passage of Scripture that speaks to you personally, and memorize it. During the Moving Toward Maturity series, concentrate on memorizing the verses as they are assigned. You will find specific steps to Scripture memorization on page 130.

BIBLE RESPONSE SHEET

DATE _____

PASSAGE _____

TITLE _____

KEY VERSE _____

SUMMARY _____

_____

_____

_____

_____

_____

PERSONAL APPLICATION _____

_____

_____

_____

_____

_____

READ THE PASSAGE SEVERAL TIMES. First read it silently, and then aloud.

UNDERSTAND THE PASSAGE.
 Read it in the context of the passages around it.
Read the comments about the verse in a Bible commentary (for example, *Wycliffe Bible Commentary*).
Write in a few words what the passage is about.

VISUALIZE THE PASSAGE. Use your imagination to picture the passage. For example, Matthew 5:1-12 is part of the "Sermon on the Mount." Picture yourself there on the mountain with Jesus. Then place each of these "Beatitudes" on the side of the mountain. Later, that picture will come to mind and help you recall these verses.

BREAK DOWN THE PASSAGE INTO NATURAL PHRASES. Learn the first phrase of the passage; then add the second. Continue adding phrases until you have memorized the entire passage.

LEARN THE REFERENCE AS PART OF THE PASSAGE. Say the reference, then the verse, and then repeat the reference again at the end. This step helps you fix the location of the verse in your mind, allowing you to turn to it immediately when you need it.

LEARN IT WORD PERFECT. As you are saying the passage over and over to yourself, continue to correct yourself until you've learned it exactly as it is written. You are already taking the time to learn it, so why not do it right! Learning it this way now will give you confidence to quote and use the passage later.

MEDITATE ON THE PASSAGE. As you think and pray about the passage, ask God to speak to you. When the passage becomes meaningful to you, then it will be much easier for you to remember.

REVIEW THE PASSAGE. Each day, review the Scripture passages you have already learned. If you review a passage every day for 30 days, it will be very difficult to forget.

PRAYER ACTION SHEET

Date _____

PRAISE:
Write down one reason to praise the Lord today.

_____

_____

THANKSGIVING:
Write down what you are most thankful for today.

_____

_____

CONFESSION:
Write down any sin(s) you need to confess.

_____

_____

Write down a promise you can claim.

_____

_____

PETITION:
Write down any needs you have in your life today.

_____

_____

INTERCESSION:
Write the names of the people you are praying for today
and a phrase that expresses your prayer for each person.

Name   Prayer

_____   _____

_____   _____

THIRTY DAYS OF PRAISE

Day 1: Psalm 8
Day 2: Psalm 23
Day 3: Psalm 34:1-3; 50:1-6
Day 4: Psalm 63:1-4; 66:1-7
Day 5: Psalm 67
Day 6: Psalm 84
Day 7: Psalm 86
Day 8: Psalm 90
Day 9: Psalm 91
Day 10: Psalm 92
Day 11: Psalm 93
Day 12: Psalm 95:1-7
Day 13: Psalm 96
Day 14: Psalm 100
Day 15: Psalm 103

Day 16: Psalm 104:1-23
Day 17: Psalm 104:24-35
Day 18: Psalm 111
Day 19: Psalm 112
Day 20: Psalm 113
Day 21: Psalm 134
Day 22: Psalm 135:1-7
Day 23: Psalm 138
Day 24: Psalm 139
Day 25: Psalm 145
Day 26: Psalm 146
Day 27: Psalm 147
Day 28: Psalm 148
Day 29: Psalm 149
Day 30: Psalm 150

SEVEN DAYS OF THANKSGIVING

Focus your thanks to the Lord in two areas each day: (1) Bible passages that describe His promises and gifts to you, and (2) your personal thanks for God's working in your daily life.

Day 1
Pray through 2 Peter 1:4 to express your thanks to God.

Lord, thank You for Your great and precious promises that You have given to me that I might be part of Your divine nature.

I also thank You for:
     Your amazing love,
     letting me be in Your family,
     making me really live, and
     life at its most fantastic in Jesus.

132

Day 2
Pray through 1 John 1:7 and Colossians 1:14 to express your thanks to God.

Father, I thank You for the blood of Your Son Jesus Christ that cleanses me from all sin and frees me from Satan's power.

I also thank You for:
    Your patience,
    Your comfort,
    Your closeness to me,
    Your disciplining of me, and
    Your love inside me.

Day 3
Pray through 1 Peter 2:24 to express your thanks to God.

Lord Jesus, I thank You that You bore my sins in Your body on the cross, so that I can die to sin and live righteously, and that by Your wounds I am healed.

I also thank You for:
    the body of Christ (other Christians),
    the privilege of prayer,
    my home, and
    my parents.

Day 4
Pray through Ephesians 2:8-10 to express your thanks to God.

Lord, I thank You that I am saved by grace through faith, and that it is Your free gift—I don't have to work for it. But thank You that, as Your new creation, I can live for You and help others.

I also thank You for:
    my body,
    my health,
    my strength,
    happy times,
    sad times, and
    in-between times.

Day 5
Pray through Psalm 91:11-14 to express your thanks to God.

Lord, I thank You that You give Your angels charge over me to guard me in all my ways. They will steady me with their hands and protect me. You will deliver me because I love You.

I also thank You for:
   opportunities for spiritual growth,
   comfort when I'm depressed,
   joy when I'm sad, and
   courage when I'm scared.

Day 6
Pray through Ephesians 1:3-6 to express your thanks to God.

Lord, thank You for choosing me to be adopted into Your family. Thank You for blessing me with all the good things You have stored up for those who belong to Christ

I also thank You for:
   food,
   clothes,
   a place to live,
   freedom to say what I feel, and
   freedom not to say what I feel.

Day 7
Pray through 2 Corinthians 8:9 and 9:8 to express your thanks to God.

Thank You, Lord, for paying a debt for me (my debt of sin) that I could never have repaid. Thank You not only for saving me from sin but for giving me the grace I need today to live for You.

I also thank You for:
   saving me from selfishness,
   saving me from pride, and
   saving me from eternal separation from You.

THIRTY DAYS OF CONFESSION

Sins to Confess:

Day 1: 2 Timothy 2:22. Do you have impure thoughts?
Day 2: Philippians 2:14-15. Do you complain or gripe?
Day 3: Ephesians 6:1-3. Do you honor your parents?
Day 4: Ephesians 4:31. Are you bitter toward anyone?
Day 5: 1 Corinthians 6:19-20. Are you careless with your body?
Day 6: Matthew 6:33. Do you seek what God wants first?
Day 7: Matthew 6:14. Do you have a bad attitude toward someone?
Day 8: 2 Timothy 2:22. Do you have impure motives?
Day 9: Colossians 3:9. Do you lie?
Day 10: Ephesians 6:1-3. Do you respect your parents?
Day 11: Ephesians 4:31. Is there anger in your life?
Day 12: 1 Corinthians 6:19-20. Do you have bad habits?
Day 13: Matthew 6:33. Is God the most important person in your life?
Day 14: Matthew 6:14. Are you holding a grudge?
Day 15: 2 Timothy 2:22. Are your thoughts pure toward the opposite sex?
Day 16: Philippians 2:14-15. Do you have a critical attitude?
Day 17: Colossians 3:9. Do you steal?
Day 18: Ephesians 4:31. Do you talk about others behind their backs?
Day 19: 1 Corinthians 6:19-20. Are you lazy?
Day 20: Matthew 6:33. Have you given God everything in your life?
Day 21: Matthew 6:14. Do you have a wrong relationship with someone?
Day 22: Colossians 3:9. Do you cheat in school?
Day 23: Ephesians 6:1-3. Do you have problems with authority?
Day 24: Ephesians 4:31. Are you jealous of anyone?
Day 25: 1 Corinthians 6:19-20. Do you eat too much?
Day 26: Matthew 6:33. Are you trusting God with your life?
Day 27: Matthew 6:14. Is there anyone you resent?
Day 28: Philippians 2:14-15. Does your attitude honor God?
Day 29: Ephesians 6:1-3. Are you rebellious?
Day 30: Ephesians 4:31. Do you argue with other people?

Promises to Claim:

Day 1: Philippians 4:8
Day 2: Psalm 119:9
Day 3: Colossians 3:9-10
Day 4: Galatians 2:20
Day 5: Colossians 3:20
Day 6: 1 John 4:7
Day 7: Hebrews 12:15
Day 8: Ephesians 4:29
Day 9: 1 Corinthians 6:13
Day 10: Colossians 1:27
Day 11: Luke 9:23
Day 12: 2 Corinthians 9:8
Day 13: 1 John 4:4
Day 14: Philippians 1:9
Day 15: 2 Thessalonians 1:12

Day 16: 1 Corinthians 10:13
Day 17: 1 Thessalonians 4:3
Day 18: Ephesians 2:10
Day 19: Colossians 1:13
Day 20: Ephesians 6:2
Day 21: Galatians 5:18
Day 22: Ephesians 4:26
Day 23: 1 Corinthians 3:16
Day 24: Romans 12:1
Day 25: 2 Corinthians 5:17
Day 26: Philippians 2:5-7
Day 27: Matthew 6:12
Day 28: Ephesians 1:3-7
Day 29: Colossians 2:2-3
Day 30: Philippians 3:1

These sins to confess and promises to claim will help you through your first 30 days of confession. During the first month, you will discover several areas God wants to change in your life. From then on, follow the passage that corresponds to that day of the month. Apply it to a sin you need to confess or promise you need to claim.

SEVEN DAYS OF PETITION

Focus your petitions in two areas each day: (1) Bible passages that describe what God wants for you, and (2) your personal requests for God to supply your needs.

DAY 1
(Read Galatians 2:20.)
"Jesus, help me to live as someone who is dead to my own selfish desires. Take charge of my body, my mind, and my emotions. Live Your life in me today."

Other needs: _____

DAY 2
(Read Galatians 5:22-23.)
"Jesus, please help my life to express these qualities to other people."

Other needs: _____

DAY 3
(Read Ephesians 5:18.)
"Jesus, I claim the filling of Your Spirit. Fill me now. I pray for all that comes from Your Spirit: courage, power, wisdom, sexual purity, boldness, compassion, enthusiasm, honesty, and openness."

Other needs: _____

DAY 4
(Read 1 Corinthians 12:4-6.)
"Lord, help me to know my spiritual gift(s) and use it for Your glory."

Other needs: _____

DAY 5
(Read Ephesians 6:10-17.)
"Jesus, it's tough to be a Christian in this world. The pressure gets heavy at times. I ask for Your strength and protection. I put on Your armor: the belt of truth, the breastplate of righteousness, the shoes of the Gospel of peace, the shield of faith, the helmet of salvation, and the sword of the Spirit—the Word of God."

Other needs: _____

DAY 6
(Read Isaiah 41:10.)
"Lord, sometimes I am afraid. But I know I don't have to get scared because You are my help and my strength. Help me today to overcome fear by trusting in You."

Other needs: _____

DAY 7
(Read Acts 1:8.)
"Jesus, I want to be a witness for You to my friends. Give me the power and courage to be Your witness today."

Other needs: _____

RECORD OF PETITION

As you begin to pray for yourself, use a form like the one below to: (1) record the things you are praying for, and (2) help you keep up with God's answers to those prayers.

NEEDS FOR MY LIFE

Date Prayed	Request	Answer	Date Answered

RECORD OF INTERCESSION

As you begin to pray for other people, use a form like the one below to: (1) record the things you are praying for each person, and (2) help you keep up with God's answers to your prayers. Fill in the person's name at the top (Mom, Dad, sister, brother, friend, etc.). Don't try to pray for everyone every day—just a few people each day is enough.

Name _____

Date Prayed	Request	Answer	Date Answered

PRAYERS YOU CAN PRAY FOR OTHERS

Look at these prayers of the Apostle Paul. They will help you know how to pray for other people. In fact, you can pray these specific prayers for them.

"And this is my prayer: that your love may abound more and more in knowledge and depth of insight, so that you may be able to discern what is best and may be pure and blameless until the day of Christ, filled with the fruit of righteousness that comes through Jesus Christ—to the glory and praise of God" (Philippians 1:9-11).

"I pray that out of His glorious riches He may strengthen you with power through His Spirit in your inner being, so that Christ may dwell in your hearts through faith. And I pray that you, being rooted and established in love, may have power, together with all the saints, to grasp how wide and long and high and deep is the love of Christ, and to know this love that surpasses knowledge—that you may be filled to the measure of all the fullness of God" (Ephesians 3:16-19).

"We always thank God for all of you, mentioning you in our prayers. We continually remember before our God and Father your work produced by faith, your labor prompted by love, and your endurance inspired by hope in our Lord Jesus Christ" (1 Thessalonians 1:2-3).

Each memory verse on these cards is printed in the *New International Version* (NIV) and in the *King James Version* (KJV). The verses correspond with the Bible studies in this book. Cut out the cards and packet along the solid black lines. Make the packet, insert the cards, and follow the instructions on the packet. ENJOY THE BENEFITS OF SCRIPTURE MEMORIZATION!

2. GROWING CLOSER 2 Tim. 3:16 (NIV)
All Scripture is God-breathed and is useful for teaching, rebuking, correcting, and training in righteousness.

1. MEETING GOD Mark 1:35 (NIV)
Very early in the morning, while it was still dark, Jesus got up, left the house and went off to a solitary place, where He prayed.

3. BIBLE STUDY Joshua 1:8 (NIV)
Do not let this Book of the Law depart from your mouth; meditate on it day and night, so that you may be careful to do everything written in it. Then you will be prosperous and successful.

4. BIBLE MEMORY Ps. 119:9-11 (NIV)
How can a young man keep his way pure? By living according to Your Word. I seek You with all my heart; do not let me stray from Your commands. I have hidden Your Word in my heart that I might not sin against You.

5. PRAYER John 15:7 (NIV)
If you remain in Me and My words remain in you, ask whatever you wish, and it will be given you.

6. PRAISE Psalm 146:1-2 (NIV)
Praise the Lord. Praise the Lord, O my soul. I will praise the Lord all my life; I will sing praise to my God as long as I live.

2. GROWING CLOSER *2 Tim. 3:16 (KJV)*
All Scripture is given by inspiration of God, and is profitable for doctrine, for reproof, for correction, for instruction in righteousness.

1. MEETING GOD *Mark 1:35 (KJV)*
And in the morning, rising up a great while before day, He went out, and departed into a solitary place, and there prayed.

3. BIBLE STUDY *Joshua 1:8 (KJV)*
This book of the law shall not depart out of thy mouth; but thou shalt meditate therein day and night, that thou mayest observe to do according to all that is written therein; for then thou shalt make thy way prosperous, and then thou shalt have good success.

4. BIBLE MEMORY *Ps. 119:9-11 (KJV)*
Wherewithal shall a young man cleanse his way? By taking heed thereto according to Thy Word. With my whole heart have I sought Thee; O let me not wander from Thy commandments. Thy word have I hid in mine heart, that I might not sin against Thee.

5. PRAYER *John 15:7 (KJV)*
If ye abide in Me and My words abide in you, ye shall ask what ye will, and it shall be done unto you.

6. PRAISE *Psalm 146:1-2 (KJV)*
Praise ye the Lord. Praise the Lord, O my soul. While I live will I praise the Lord: I will sing praises unto my God while I have any being.

142

7. THANKSGIVING
1 Thessalonians 5:18 (NIV)
Give thanks in all circumstances, for this is God's will for you in Christ Jesus.

8. CONFESSION   1 John 1:9 (NIV)
If we confess our sins, He is faithful and just and will forgive us our sins and purify us from all unrighteousness.

9. PETITION   Matthew 7:7-8 (NIV)
Ask and it will be given to you; seek and you will find; knock and the door will be opened to you. For everyone who asks receives; he who seeks finds; and to him who knocks, the door will be opened.

10. INTERCESSION
2 Corinthians 10:4-5 (NIV)
The weapons we fight with are not the weapons of the world. On the contrary, they have divine power to demolish strongholds. We demolish arguments and every pretension that sets itself up against the knowledge of God, and we take captive every thought to make it obedient to Christ.

PACKET ➤ Cut out.
FOR ➤ Fold *in* on dotted lines.
CARDS ➤ Tape short flap to back on outside edges.

INSTRUCTIONS:

▲ Always carry this packet with you.
▲ Memorize a verse a week.
▲ Daily review each verse you've learned.
▲ Have someone check your progress each week.
▲ Apply each verse to your daily life.

SPENDING TIME
ALONE WITH GOD
Bible Memory Packet

7. THANKSGIVING
1 Thessalonians 5:18 (KJV)
In every thing give thanks: for this is the will of God in Christ Jesus concerning you.

8. CONFESSION   *1 John 1:9 (KJV)*
If we confess our sins, He is faithful and just to forgive us our sins, and to cleanse us from all unrighteousness.

9. PETITION   *Matthew 7:7-8 (KJV)*
Ask, and it shall be given you; seek, and ye shall find; knock, and it shall be opened unto you: For every one that asketh receiveth; and he that seeketh findeth; and to him that knocketh it shall be opened.

10. INTERCESSION
2 Corinthians 10:4-5 (KJV)
(For the weapons of our warfare are not carnal, but mighty through God to the pulling down of strong holds;) Casting down imaginations, and every high thing that exalteth itself against the knowledge of God, and bringing into captivity every thought to the obedience of Christ.